Heroes In Heels

Ignite Your Soul and Awaken the Hero Within

A 30-DAY JOURNEY

To Natalie,
Here's to the Hero Within!.
Enjoy the journey...
much love,

Heroes In Heels

Ignite Your Soul and Awaken the Hero Within

A 30-DAY JOURNEY

CARRIE FLINTOM

**With Contributions
by Pam Rundquist**

Langdon Street Press
212 3rd Avenue North, Suite 290
Minneapolis, MN 55401
612.455.2293
www.langdonstreetpress.com

ISBN - 978-1-934938-38-6
ISBN - 1-934938-38-6
LCCN - 2009923171

Book sales for North America and international:
Itasca Books, 3501 Highway 100 South, Suite 220
Minneapolis, MN 55416
Phone: 952.345.4488 (toll free 1.800.901.3480)
Fax: 952.920.0541; email to orders@itascabooks.com

Cover Design by Tiffany Laschinger
Typeset by James Arneson

Printed in the United States of America

LANGDON STREET PRESS

CONTENTS

DEDICATION

*T*his book is dedicated to all the heroic women who, through their loving support, elevate and enrich the lives of others. Thank you for your love, courage, selflessness, and determination. May this book provide inspiration and an awakening to all the women still on their journey to find the Hero within.

AUTHOR'S NOTE

*T*hroughout this book are stories from women sharing personal extraordinary moments and experiences with other women. All the contributors have granted permission to use their stories in this book. Some names have been changed by request to protect individual privacy.

I am profoundly grateful to these women who put their trust in me to share their unique and intimate experiences. I was touched by every story that found its way to me and felt deeply inspired by the love and support that was given by each woman in these beautiful moments.

FOREWORD

It is better to light a candle than to curse the darkness.
~ Anonymous

A pivotal moment in my garage forever changed my life. The unexpected but extraordinary event was the day I experienced a genuine awakening.

I had just dropped my three children off at school and was on automatic pilot driving up Discovery Way, the street where I lived. Just as I had done a thousand times, I pulled my big red Expedition into the garage of my comfortable suburban home and slowly removed the key from the ignition. But this time, instead of getting out of the car, I sat frozen. It seemed as if, for a brief moment, the world stopped. I felt paralyzed as I sat staring through my windshield into an empty, dark, garage wall. The quiet still-small voice in my head spoke loud and clear, posing the question that would unexpectedly re-shape my life. "How did I get here?" Not "How did I get into my garage?" but "How did my life get to this place?" Like most women, I was incredibly busy with all the details and demands that I had created and accepted through the years. I loved my life and being a mom more than anything in the world, but somehow, somewhere along the way, I found myself lost – and, amazingly enough, I was lost within my own life.

I had everything that should make me happy, I thought. I enjoyed the many roles and titles I had been called through the years: wife, mother, daughter, sister, friend, coach, assistant, art lady, neighbor, co-worker, and obedient church member, to name a few. The process of losing myself transpired slowly, one title and one small demand or acquired duty at a time. In retrospect, the more titles and responsibilities I attained over the years, the more I disconnected from my true authentic self. Like millions of other women, I struggled to be everything to everyone in my life. At the same time, I found myself trapped in a world of unforeseen contradictions. Now, at this stage of my life, I was tremendously overwhelmed, but bored by the daily routine. I was married, but I felt painfully lonely. I suffered from exhaustion, but often felt preoccupied and apprehensive. I was a "Supermom," but I was running on a tank that was super-empty. Like so many, I was "religious," but not "spiritual." In every snapshot that showcased our home, I smiled broadly, but I frequently cried alone in the bathtub at night.

On that day, in my dark garage, for whatever reason, all these contradictions abruptly came to light, suddenly, and right out of the blue. There I was, sitting in a parked car, my life a confusing mess. Like an overflowing river bursting through a worn-out levee, a flood of tears began to pour out of me, as the uncomfortable truth could no longer be ignored or denied. Simply stated, I became conscious of the bitter fact that, behind all the roles and responsibilities, I truly had no idea who I was anymore. Even worse, I realized I was sleepwalking through my own life.

As I began to share this "ah-ha" moment with my family and friends, I came to the conclusion that quite a few of the women I knew were paralyzed with similar feelings. We were all running in a multitude of directions, so much so that we struggled to find time to share a cup of coffee with each other or carve out an hour to simply take a short walk together. Regrettably, though we were always running, we rarely seemed to be running toward our own personal joy and fulfillment.

With this new awakening and blossoming awareness, I began the uneasy search to rediscover my life. I read and listened to any and all experts who offered insight into how to get my life back. The process was exhilarating. Each "master" offered remarkable advice and direction on how to find what I was urgently searching for: ME!

As best I could, I applied each expert's strategies and tools with dedication and passion and began to feel a new strength and energy within. When I finished reading one book, I immediately moved to another, and then another. Soon, I was combining various techniques to live a purpose-filled, passionate, and fulfilling life. Finally, I found the right combination of key components that I could practically and consistently incorporate in my challenging schedule. In doing so, I not only re-connected with my soul, I discovered a new and authentic life purpose.

During this extraordinary process of awakening and re-claiming my life, it was the women in my life who made the most profound impact on my evolution, both positively and negatively. I was genuinely inspired by, and grateful for, the strength, support, and love that were freely given by many remarkable women. (My true Heroes in Heels!) Conversely, I was disillusioned and saddened by some women who tried to devalue me for daring to want more. I was completely taken aback by hurtful gossip and judgment fed to the community about me as I made the terrifyingly difficult and necessary changes (including leaving my marriage) to achieve the happiness and fulfillment that my soul desperately needed. This experience, though extremely painful, taught me important and invaluable lessons about friendship and women. The truth is that we all have an impact on the women with whom we come in contact and with those we have close relationships. Whether we choose to be an empowering or demeaning influence, we make a difference in all our relationships.

What follows in these pages is the culmination of knowledge and life skills I have learned, applied and been helped by in searching for my own authentic self. This book honors all the heroic women who, day after day, continuously travel life's unique and challenging journey with all the titles and responsibilities borne valiantly, but who, like me, may have lost their authentic and purposeful life somewhere along the way.

With all my heart I believe women need to come together as one. To reach our fulfillment we must consciously stop backstabbing, judging, and gossiping about each other. We must intentionally dare to show love for each other. Never before in history have women taken on so many roles and have had such demanding lives. More importantly, it's now our responsibility as women to pull together, love each other, support each other and embrace each of our unique and remarkable life missions.

The examples in this book are from ordinary women sharing extraordinary experiences. In their own moments of heartache or challenge they found miracles in the faces of women who stepped up to be their guardians. It is within these small but decisive moments that true heroes are made. With each opportunity, these courageous women reached greater heights, choosing the unrivaled and oftentimes more difficult path. To find and use their light, they had to look inward. So it is with you and me.

It is with great joy that I invite you to share this journey. I hope your heart will be touched, that you will be challenged to live more passionately, and feel inspired to reach out to empower yourself and those around you.

Carrie Flintom

INTRODUCTION

In each of us are heroes; speak to them and they will come forth.
~Eleanor Roosevelt

$\mathcal{M}$ore than ever before, women's lives are escalating into a vastly complicated existence. We find ourselves continually burdened with more responsibilities and demands, while existing in an exceedingly competitive culture that will manipulate every component of our lives if we let it. Sadly, we sometimes disconnect with ourselves and with other women because of this demanding lifestyle and spirited competition. We often step on each other in our attempt to climb the corporate ladder, raise successful kids, nurture our relationships or cope with divorce. We feel pressure to strive (or tragically, starve) to emulate the airbrushed magazine-cover bodies that are, literally, unattainable.

We stumble in our struggle to stay on target with the ideal image society refers to as "Today's Woman." Consequently, if we aren't performing successfully on all levels, we frequently sense failure. At the same time, we award ourselves with an appropriate measure of guilt.

- Guilt for not spending enough time with our kids (or significant other) due to work demands.
- Guilt for spending too much on material items for our kids to compensate for the guilt of not being there for them enough.
- Guilt for letting our jobs slide when we focus on our families at the expense of our workplace.
- Guilt for putting the relationship with our significant other at the bottom of the list.
- Guilt for breaking up our family when a marriage "fails."
- Guilt for not being healthy and fit when we can't seem to carve out any extra time, let alone energy, to go to the gym or exercise regularly.

Life for many women is a springboard into a bottomless sea of frustration and disappointment. So many women are not just treading in distress; they are drowning. Balancing all these demands can be overwhelming at times. "Having it all" with regard to work, motherhood, marriage, and more is, in many ways, expected; anything less is below par. In the struggle to "have it all," we often lose our identities for a period in our lives. We are left feeling fragmented, unsatisfied, and overwhelmed.

We say we want it all – but do we really? Are we even clear about what the "it" is that we want? And how does "it" feed and nourish our souls?

Now more than ever, women need to join forces to sustain each other, reinforce each other, consult and listen to each other, and, most important, love each other. We need other women to encourage us, edify us, lift our spirits and help us discover ways to embrace the magic in our complicated lives while learning to survive the demanding challenges we face daily.

Women can help define each other in profound ways. When we give to others, that love helps dissolve the boundaries of separation and connects us to a sense of belonging. We each have something special to offer and contribute. When we are in a position to assist someone, we have an invaluable opportunity.

With every encounter, we are given the chance to touch an individual life and, in doing so, nourish our own spirit, awaken our highest self and make our mark in this world. But do we do it? Again, in most cases, we find the answer to be a resounding "no." Despite the challenges we all face, women can discover genuine joy and live a harmonious life every day. This book presents a systematic daily approach that is designed to stimulate personal breakthroughs and support internal transformations that make possible a fulfilling and purpose-filled life.

Welcome to *Heroes in Heels* - a message for today's women who, whether trying to balance everyday demands in five-inch stilettos or racing around town in worn-out athletic shoes, squander way-too-much time feeling overwhelmed, unfulfilled, restless, confused, and disappointed. Imagine waking up every morning fully alive, with gratitude in your heart, inspired and excited to get on with your objective and intention. Imagine how it would it feel to place your head on the pillow every night completely fulfilled, celebrating a sense of purpose and passion.

Come, join in a unique and magical experience. Learn the difference between searching for the meaning of life, and creating it for yourself. Life's meaning can be found everywhere we encounter relationships. Seemingly unimportant encounters can become extremely powerful when we approach these "small moments" with a new, insightful vision. These are the moments when the ordinary life becomes extraordinary. These are the moments we can become heroes.

In the next thirty days, together we will explore, experiment, reveal the essence of our purpose and embrace the soul and spirit of our being. Together we will live each day with gratitude, affirmations, inspiration, intention, and passion as we witness all the miracles in each other's lives, as well as our own.

It's time to become the hero of your own life. Put on your favorite "heels," and let's begin the journey!

Chapter 1

THE 30-DAY JOURNEY

...and then the day came when the risk to remain tight in a bud was more painful than the risk it took to blossom.

~ Anais Nin

*I*n creating this 30-day journey, every effort was made to create a simple, daily system to reinforce the synchronicity that drew you to pick up this book in the first place. Each element is an important ingredient for the recipe of success in a daily life of love and fulfillment. This uncomplicated process is intended to guide you and keep you focused in all your efforts. Here's the formula:

- Each day begins with a brief personal story shared by a woman who performed an act of kindness toward another women or who was the recipient of an act of kindness. May these true stories touch your heart and <u>inspire</u> you to go out and make a difference that day.
- Next a <u>motivating</u> quotation is provided to set the tone for your day.
- An <u>affirmation</u> is provided to help direct your <u>intention</u> for your day.

- You are asked to take a moment to acknowledge and record your gratitude for the day.
- Finally, you are asked to journal (at the end of your day) about the act of love you gave (your "Heroic Moment") as well as record your feelings after sharing this gift.

In following this easy format, you will truly begin to create the wonderful life of love and happiness you desire. If you have some difficulty getting started and need a "boost" of ideas and examples of acts of love you can try, one hundred "Booster Shots" are provided in the back of the book.

By the end of this thirty-day journey, you will have formed wonderful new habits, learned a magnificent, fresh way of expressing yourself in this world and will have profoundly touched at least thirty lives that otherwise might not have been touched. The world will be different because of your love, and you will enjoy feeling more love and joy than you could have possibly imagined--simply by giving ONE act of love each day.

To understand the power of each element in the daily process, we will explain in detail each course of action that binds this system together, and why the daily process in this format works.

Chapter 2

THE POWER OF AFFIRMATIONS

It's the repetition of affirmations that leads to belief. And once that belief becomes a deep conviction, things will begin to happen.
~ Claude M Bristol

*M*any of us grew up learning to put ourselves down or comparing ourselves to others. We often unconsciously demean ourselves by saying self-condemning statements, such as, "I hate my life," or "I'm not good enough." It is too common within the human condition that many of us have learned to be negative rather than positive. These statements are based on our beliefs, what we often create in our minds and accept as our own truths or reality. It is critical that, for us to have positive growth in our lives, we replace these dysfunctional beliefs with positive ones.

An affirmation is a declaration that something is true. Short, positive statements, focused on a specific set of beliefs, remind us to think consciously about our thoughts and words. The concept and use of affirmations for self-improvement changes the negative self-talk in our heads to positive self-talk. Using affirmations as a daily exercise will help reprogram your thought patterns, and change the way you think and feel about things. They will help ground your purpose and help keep you focused on your intention.

In her book, *You Can Heal Your Life*, Louise L. Hay, an internationally renowned author and speaker on personal growth and self-healing, explains how our beliefs and ideas about ourselves are often the cause of our emotional problems and even our physical troubles. She believes that by using certain powerful tools such as affirmations, we can change our thinking and our lives for the better. She states, "Affirmations are like little reminder notes to the inner-self. Affirmations are always positive and harness the power of positive thinking to keep the inner self on track!"

Affirmations are most powerful when they are emotionally charged. Say them with passion! The higher the emotional state, the more effective they will be in your life. One of the best ways to evoke a strong feeling of belief when stating an affirmation is to express gratitude after you recite the affirmation, as if it's already happened. Saying "thank you" reinforces the belief that the universe has already fulfilled your desires and intentions.

Chapter 3

THE POWER OF INTENTION

Everything that you want -- all the joy, love, abundance, prosperity, bliss -- it's there, ready for you to grab a hold of it. And you've got to get hungry for it. You've got to be intentional. And when you become intentional and on fire for what you want, the Universe will deliver every single thing that you've been wanting.
~ Lisa Nichols (The Secret)

*Y*our intentions have brought you to where you are today. Your actions always eventually mirror your thoughts. If you change your intentions, you can change your position in life. We learn from quantum physics that everything in our universe is made up of energy. This law operates with or without our conscious attention, belief, or understanding. If you want to achieve any goal or desire, you must first decide to make it happen. Once you make a clear, committed decision about what you want, the universal energy attracts that into your life. Even if you can't see how something will come about, don't worry about the how; simply focus and declare your intention, and the universe will find a way to make it happen.

Putting this concept into practice might take some time for you to see how it works in your life. But if you truly state your intention, and trust the law of intention, you will begin to see the power you have to bring whatever you want into your life. If you want to find an opportunity to help someone today, then intend it to happen and watch who shows up in your day. You need to be consciously open to recognize the opportunities that present themselves to you. Someone is most likely not going to come up to you and say, "I need help, can you help me?" Be aware of the quiet whispers throughout your day, and you will begin to recognize your intentions in action.

Chapter 4

THE POWER OF GRATITUDE

Gratitude unlocks the fullness of life. It turns what we have into enough, and more. It turns denial into acceptance, chaos into order, and confusion into clarity. It turns problems into gifts, failures into success, the unexpected into perfect timing, and mistakes into important events. Gratitude makes sense of our past, brings peace for today and creates a vision for tomorrow.
~ Melodie Beattie

*G*ratitude is a powerful energy force for creating immense joy in your life. Being grateful opens your heart and allows the space to attract more of whatever you want in life. As you experience and participate in feeling grateful on a daily basis, you begin to notice that all the things that you have to be thankful for are the cornerstones of prosperity.

To feel grateful is not to imply that everything in our lives is essentially great. Gratitude means that we are consciously aware of all the blessings we currently enjoy. It means that we are looking at life through the eyes of appreciation and thankfulness instead of through the eyes of fear. When this visual shift takes place, you will be amazed at how different the world looks, even though nothing changed other than your view of it. As Dr. Wayne Dyer beautifully explains in his book, *The Power of Intention,* "When you change the way you look at things, the things you look at begin to change."

You're very first thought in the morning (even before your feet touch the ground!) should be of all that you are grateful for. Be thankful for the new day and all its possibilities, your health, your family, your pet, your friends. Starting every day with a feeling of gratitude will lay the groundwork and set the tone for how you will experience the rest of your day. Put yourself in a state of gratitude and you will begin to notice simple blessings all around you, and how many people touch your life every day. But more importantly, many opportunities to produce a "Heroic Moment" will present themselves to you. The quiet whispers are the pathways that lead you to the miraculous possibilities for profound change in your life.

Chapter 5

THE POWER OF ACTION

We learn to speak by speaking, to study by studying, to run by running, to work by working; and just so, you learn to love by loving. All those who think in any other way deceive themselves.
~ Saint Francis De Sales

*T*ransforming your thoughts into reality begins by taking some positive action. Change is always possible, at any time, no matter where you are in life. Change is the essential ingredient to any growth. There comes a time in all our lives when we have to decide if we are going to stay as we have been, or reach a new height and become someone new, someone better. The moment you decide to truly change is a moment that you will move your life in a forward direction.

When you put into action your intentions and desires, the shift will occur that begins the process of developing the new habits that will form the new beginning of how you experience life on a daily basis. The beauty in giving is that the universe works to give you back more than you have sown. You will always win when you give. On the other hand, if you hold back from the universe, you will reap what you sow. Energy needs to be in motion or it becomes stagnant. As Deepak Chopra states in his book, *The 7 Spiritual Laws of Success,* "The more you give, the more you will receive, because you will keep the abundance of the universe circulating in your life. In fact, anything that is of value in life only multiplies when it is given."

Think love, talk about love, read about love, write about love, and give love, and love will wrap itself around you like you've never known.

Chapter 6

THE POWER OF JOURNALING

Each thought that is welcomed and recorded is a nest egg, by the side of which more will be laid. Thoughts accidentally thrown together become a frame in which more may be developed and exhibited. Perhaps this is the main value of a habit of writing, or keeping a journal – that so we remember our best hours and stimulate ourselves.
~ Henry David Thoreau

*I*f you've ever enjoyed the benefits of writing your thoughts and intentions, you know why this is a key element in producing results. If you haven't, then you are in for an awakening and powerful new experience. Writing down your thoughts can open up a new understanding of what you can achieve in life and give you a clearer perspective of what is going on in your thinking patterns, which is very important. When you write down your thoughts, feelings, ideas, goals, and experiences, you send that energy and those messages out into the universe in a different more powerful form. This process will help you stay focused in your endeavors, give you insight to what you're experiencing and, finally, give you the opportunity to review your entries, chronicling how much you've grown, as well as gaining insight to the successes you've achieved during this process.

Oftentimes, through putting your thoughts and goals on paper, you can release ideas and feelings that you might not even be consciously aware of. The beauty of journaling is that there are no rules. There's no wrong or right way to do it. You have the opportunity to simply let what is in your heart and mind flow out of you. In the blank pages ahead, you will not only write your experiences, but more importantly, you will make the connection to how you can write your future. We truly write our own life stories. So why not write the best story possible? When you write what you want, you will be amazed how the universe aligns itself to create and support just that.

"Come to the edge," he said.
They said, "We are afraid."
"Come to the edge," he said.
They came.
He pushed them...
And they flew.

-Guilluame Apollinaire

THE JOURNEY BEGINS...

Day 1

MABEL AND THE LILACS

by Carrie Flintom

Our day started as a typical day, two friends simply running a few errands together. No one could have guessed that the day would turn into something so remarkable. As my friend Pam and I were driving to a store, Pam noticed a beautiful lilac tree in full bloom. She nearly drove off the road as she cheered for me to look over at the blossoms' beauty. She told me that lilacs were her mom's favorite flower, and they only bloom for a short time. We decided to ask the homeowner if we could pick a few lilacs and take them to Pam's mom to brighten her day! Pam quickly pulled a U-turn and, before we knew it, we were knocking at the door of this unfamiliar home, hoping to find a kind resident willing to share their beautiful flowers. After minutes without an answer, we decided to go over to smell the lilacs. They were amazing! Before long, we rationalized our way to the decision that it would be okay to pick a few of the flowers (since it was for a good cause!).

As we were anxiously picking, a car pulled into the driveway. Pam and I glanced at each other with the "uh-oh!" look, hoping the owners would not come after us with baseball bats. We quickly saw that the people were an elderly couple. The loving husband was carefully helping his wife out of the noticeably old Chevrolet.

She was a petite African-American woman who appeared frail, clearly struggling to walk and evidently in a great deal of pain. They smiled curiously at us as we approached them with the flowers in our hands.

Within minutes of explaining what we were doing and why two crazy blonde women were in their yard picking their flowers, the charming and beautiful woman said with a delightful southern accent, "I'm so happy someone will get to enjoy them. We're so old and weak that we can't ever pick them to enjoy inside." We immediately asked if we could make a bouquet for their table. They were both thrilled and thanked us for our generosity in offering to cut the flowers for them.

The woman explained that they just returned from the hospital where she had recently undergone open-heart surgery. She explained that it had been quite an arduous few months. Pam and I were immediately touched by this woman's spirit. There was something extraordinary about her. We found ourselves intrigued with her strength. Her name was Mabel, and we were friends from the moment we met her. She was trapped in a sick-ridden, worn, fragile body, but had one of the strongest spirits we had ever encountered. We shared engaging conversation with Mabel and her husband for quite a while before determining that we should leave so that Mabel could get her much-needed rest.

As we said goodbye to Mabel and her husband, she said in a very matter-of-fact tone, "You two must be sisters." We explained that we were not sisters, but that we each came from families where we had two older brothers and no sister, so we had become each other's sister. She paused and gazed at us for a long moment, and then smiled and said with an assertive, yet tender, voice, "You two are sisters under the skin; I can see that." Both Pam and I had goose bumps as we looked at each other and replied, "You're right! We truly are *sisters under the skin!*"

We hugged our new beautiful friend gently, making sure not to hurt her fragile body. Soon we were driving down the road to Pam's mom's house with a lovely bouquet of fresh-picked lilacs and deeply touched hearts.

We never did get to the store we were originally heading for that day. What began as a simple errand turned into a marvelous and extraordinary experience that neither Pam nor I will ever forget. Our simple intention of wanting to lift Pam's mom's day resulted in brightening an elderly couple's home with lilacs from their tree, making special new friends, lifting the spirits of Mabel and her husband, delighting Pam's mom with beautiful fresh lilacs for her kitchen table and, to top it all off, Pam and I were given the perfect and unique "naming" of our special relationship--one we refer to even now when describing our friendship.

Whenever Pam or I see lilacs in bloom, we always think of our friend Mabel and that remarkable day that brought unlikely strangers together and gave us all a few moments of unexpected joy. You never know what each seemingly ordinary day will bring, or whose life you might touch. Miracles are all around us, if we will simply remember to just stop and smell the "lilacs" once in awhile.

It is man's foremost duty to awaken the understanding of the inner self and to know his own real inner greatness. Once he knows his true worth, he can know the worth of others.
~ Swami Muktanada

AFFIRMATION

In understanding my inner self, my choice to create, I acknowledge the greatness I have been blessed with. I use this inner greatness to better the lives of those I come in contact with. Because of the love for myself, and understanding of my purpose, I am able to understand the greatness in all of mankind.

Today! I am **grateful** for:

_____

_____

_____

_____

Today! I **intend** to contribute love to the universe and share one kind act with someone I come in contact with.

Today! My **"HEROIC MOMENT"** was:

_____

_____

_____

When I shared my gift of love, I **felt:**

_____

_____

_____

Day 2

THE REAL STORY

by Pam Rundquist

*M*y father was a beautiful man. Even as a small girl this was evident to me. There was a light about him, a perfect joy. When he entered a room, people were drawn to him. I always knew my father loved me. He showered me with unconditional love and made me feel that there was absolutely nothing I couldn't do. His love encouraged me to be open to all of life's opportunities. "No regrets, no stone unturned, no coulda, woulda, shouldas."

So on that crisp, sunny day in February, as my father's spirit slipped away peacefully, I knew he had lived the life that he encouraged me to emulate. The coming weeks following his passing brought many stories, anecdotes, tender memories and, most of all, praise for a man with a life well-lived. But none of the stories touched me more than the unexpected gift that came the day we honored him at his funeral.

Janet (a somewhat familiar face) walked into the viewing room and signed the guest book. I felt an immediate sense of recognition as well as an element of surprise. Janet and I worked together twenty or so years earlier. During that period of time, and through a series of conversations, we connected the dots and realized that she knew my father. They both shared the medical diagnosis of tinnitus, a constant and incurable ringing in the ear. But that was as far as the conversations ever went at the time.

I walked toward Janet and stretched out my hand. We exchanged hellos, and I introduced her to my family. I was somewhat curious as to why she was there, and so I asked her. She proceeded to tell me she came that day to share her story of my father, the *real* story.

Many years ago, my father discovered Janet's name on a list of patients who belonged to the local tinnitus society. They frequented the same doctors, acupuncturists, holistic practitioners, and yoga and meditation specialists.

Janet told me that on many occasions my father called to encourage her, share new information with her or simply tell her to "hang in there." She explained his uncanny ability to always sense when she was having her worst day and to call. Their interaction continued through the years but, as my father entered retirement and unfortunately began the awful descent into dementia, they lost touch.

What I didn't know until that moment was that Janet had never actually met my father in person. She never met this wonderful man with whom she had enjoyed a very personal and caring relationship. My father reached out to her over the phone because time and distance kept them from meeting. I was amazed that my father so positively impacted her life, even though they never met. I paused to remember. *Yes, my father was a beautiful man, inside and out.*

Janet came to meet my father in person for the very first time at his funeral. She came to say hello, say thank you and say goodbye. She also came to see me that day, to share a very private and powerful snapshot of how my father touched her life. A story he never shared when he was alive. He was too humble of a man to recount his own kindnesses to others.

Janet said she felt inspired to come that day, as if a voice were pushing her, prodding her. I am tremendously grateful to Janet that she followed her nudge and came to share her story with me. As with most loving acts, the gift my father gave to Janet now had extended beyond her, to me. It was the hug I needed from my father as we spent that day saying goodbye.

In those few minutes, Janet gave me a gift, a legacy to hold on to, a view of love and the way my father made an impact on her life. In this offering of honest and genuine compassion, she changed my life, too.

I think about that day and imagine how it would be to have someone show up at the end of my life to tell a story about me-- *the real story*. By Janet's sharing of this beautiful story of my father, I was reminded that we rarely know how much of an impression we make on other lives we touch. I'm sure my father had no idea of the imprint he left on this woman, and how it would come back to comfort me in my time of need.

This one story about my father remains closest to my heart.

Thank you Janet, and thank you Daddy, I love you.

*We plant the seeds of love, knowing that nature will take its course
and in time those seeds will bear fruit. Some seeds will come to
fruition quickly, some slowly, but our work is simply to plant the
seeds. Every time we form the intention in the mind for our own
happiness or for the happiness of others, we are doing our work; we
are channeling the powerful energies of our own minds.*

~ Sharon Salzberg

AFFIRMATION

Today is a gift. I recognize that I am here to make a difference in the world TODAY! It is the purpose I give myself. I feel appreciation for all that I am, all I have, and all I can give; and will share with someone my appreciation for them today.

Today! I am **grateful** for:

_____

_____

_____

Today! I **intend** to contribute love to the universe and share one kind act with someone I come in contact with.

Today! My **"HEROIC MOMENT"** was:

_____

_____

_____

When I shared my gift of love, I **felt:**

_____

_____

_____

_____

_____

Day 3

HAIR TODAY, GONE TOMORROW

by Mary Jo Campbell

After several days of accelerated hair thinning (thanks to a strong chemo drug to treat my cancer) I visited my son, a gifted hairdresser, for a short haircut. Despite the deep pile accumulating on the floor, he remained positive and pleasant and took extra care to make my new look as feminine as possible. It would be months before I knew the emotional toll this event had on him. Within days, the remaining hair on my head was a botched conglomeration of random patches of short hairs. The need for a wig was imminent. Once again, family came to the rescue. My college-age daughter and her older aunt (a cancer survivor herself) embarked with me on a girls' day out to find the perfect wig. Lunch and laughter were interspersed with support and honesty in this important pursuit. Finally settling on the right wig, however, took days, not just an afternoon. When it was time to remove the rest of the hair and have a clean dome on which to perch the masterpiece, the following scene took place:

Towel – check. Razor with new blade – check. Camera – check. Courage – sure. Sense of humor – umm, we'll see. I leaned over the kitchen sink with a towel around my neck. With the water running, my daughter started at the back of my head and carefully began drawing a Venus razor over what was left of my pixie cut. It felt tickle-y, and a bit creepy, and then just tedious. Heads are lumpy with lots of curves; a pair of clippers would have worked more easily. Didn't have them. Just before finishing, we took a break. My nose was getting stuffy, my back sore and patience thin. There was a triangular swatch left where my bangs should have been and, without much coaxing, it flipped into a baby curl, turning me into an alien with a mini-pompadour. Hysterical laughter and silly poses filled the room as we captured the moment and cracked jokes.

Simultaneously, I felt a lump growing in my throat. It was official. It would be months before I'd need a blow dryer or curling iron. Where would I stop applying foundation makeup with a forehead that kept on going? I'd joined the ranks of cancer victims of all varieties, ages, and genders. Relief and resignation collided in my heart; only an act of will kept me from bursting into tears as my first "bald" pictures were taken.

It's amazing how we draw strength and perspective from one another as women. I was still "Mom," but my daughter became my part-time caregiver, doing things for me that I couldn't do myself. Her wonderful gift of encouragement was straightforward. "You honestly look better bald than with that pixie cut."

Everyone has a purpose in life…a unique gift or special talent to give to others. And when we blend this unique talent with service to others, we experience the ecstasy and exultation of our own spirit, which is the ultimate goal of all goals.
*~ **Deepak Chopra***

AFFIRMATION

I create what I want in life. Today I will ask what it is I really want out of my day, and then make it happen. It will be my own private miracle. Because I want an abundance of love in my life, I will give it to the universe, knowing it will come back to me tenfold.

Today! I am **grateful** for:

_____
_____
_____

Today! I **intend** to contribute love to the universe and share one kind act with someone I come in contact with.

Today! My **"HEROIC MOMENT"** was:

_____
_____
_____

When I shared my gift of love, I **felt**:

_____
_____
_____

Day 4

THE MASTERMIND MIRACLE

by Tamara Johnson

*W*hen my husband was in the hospital waiting for open-heart surgery, I felt tremendous stress. Trying to juggle my daughter's school schedule, continuing to work and running back and forth to the hospital, I often felt like I wasn't going to make it through this crisis. In the middle of it all, a woman in the "mastermind" group I had organized responded to my situation in a very non-compassionate way, which added to my misery.

Then, out of the blue, a dear friend from the same mastermind group called me and said, "Listen honey, I have been thinking about you and everything you are going through. I was just wondering; would a thousand dollars help you?"

I broke into tears and told her about the financial stresses I was experiencing. She said, "Well, meet me in front of Trader Joe's in one hour." I went. She handed me an envelope with ten one-hundred-dollar bills and gave me a hug. She said, "Listen, this is not a loan. Just be sure that later, when things are going better for you, you remember to pay it forward. Just help someone else who needs it."

I was unbelievably grateful. There is no way this girlfriend could have known the impact her kindness would have on my life.

Each person's smile at a particular moment constitutes
a unique event in the history of mankind.
*~ **Rene Dubos***

AFFIRMATION

My life has meaning when I embrace love and share this gift with others. Honor those who enrich your life – even if it's only in your heart and thoughts. I will choose to love not only those closest to me, but also the strangers who cross my path today. I know that a kind smile can change their entire day.

Today! I am **grateful** for:

_____
_____
_____

Today! I **intend** to contribute love to the universe and share one kind act with someone I come in contact with.

Today! My **"HEROIC MOMENT"** was:

_____
_____
_____

When I shared my gift of love, I **felt:**

_____
_____
_____

Day 5

DERBY DIVAS

by Sabrina Hackett

$\mathcal{M}$y girlfriend, Kathy Seibert-Miller, from my hometown, Louisville, fought breast cancer for more than ten years before succumbing to the disease on April 8, 2005, at the age of forty-four. Before her death, she planned her "Celebration of Life" memorial service, to be held at the Churchill Downs Kentucky Derby Museum. She wanted all her friends to wear our favorite Derby Hat and a new pair of shoes for the occasion. Kathy was well known around town for her love of horses, her hats, and her shoes.

On the day of Kathy's memorial service, I took a seat in the back row with my sister and other girlfriends, all wearing our favorite hats. From there I could see rows and rows of beautiful spring "Derby" hats. It touched me to know how happy Kathy would be that her plan came together on such a gorgeous spring day. Several words were spoken about her positive outlook on life and her fun-loving personality. But one message stood out above the rest. "Whenever you buy a new pair of shoes, figuratively or literally, step out in style with Kathy's determined positive spirit, and do something good for someone."

Upon leaving Kathy's inspirational service I immediately felt inspired to "step out in style" and "do something good for someone." With this goal in mind, I created a stylish and feminine horseracing-themed dice game to honor Kathy and the spirit of women everywhere who have fought to survive breast cancer, including my own mother who has battled the disease five times over the past twenty years. The game is called "Derby Divas" and proceeds are given to breast cancer research through our "Roll for a Cure" program. For more information, visit www.derbydivas.com.

I hope you will find my story worth sharing with other women—because it is often those who are not with us today who create impressions that last a lifetime.

When you are grateful, fear disappears and abundance appears.
~ *Tony Robbins*

AFFIRMATION

When I am filled with gratitude, I know that the windows of possibility open and I create more space for blessings, happiness, and love to come to me. Today I will focus on all that I already have instead of all the things I wish I had.

Today! I am **grateful** for:

_____

_____

_____

Today! I **intend** to contribute love to the universe and share one kind act with someone I come in contact with.

Today! My **"HEROIC MOMENT"** was:

_____

_____

_____

When I shared my gift of love, I **felt**:

_____

_____

_____

Day 6

NO SCOREBOARD
BETWEEN TRUE FRIENDS

by Katherine Eitel

I've had a "best friend" since fifth grade. We've remained close friends through marriages, divorces, babies, teenagers, college, career highs and lows, and now menopause, and the first of what we hope are many grandchildren. We've done this despite the long geographic distance between us. She lives in Michigan and I live in Southern California.

Last year, my friend didn't seem quite the same on our regular phone check-ins and finally on an actual visit to my new home, over a stiff glass of wine, she told me she had been dealing with a huge breach of trust concerning her husband (and soul mate) and one of his female psychotherapy clients in a small town where my friend is a prominent attorney. The client was bringing forth a lawsuit of grand proportion. My friend had to deal with the issue personally, and she had to face a small highly religious community, her law constituents and, very likely, she'd have to sit down and tell their grown children about it if the lawsuit went all way through the court system. My friend was heartbroken and distraught.

Next, she said she had a huge favor to ask. She wanted to be far away from her hometown during the week of the trial, in the loving circle of the only two friends on the planet who knew about this.

I told my friend I'd handle all the arrangements for an awesome week and book three flights to Sedona, AZ. I lied to my clients and made up some amazing stories about why I had to cancel the consulting engagements that had been on the books for a year. I told (didn't ask) my staff and family that I'd be gone for a week.

I researched hotels and found a European-style resort with exquisite cabins right on the pristine Sedona Creek, made reservations at the best restaurants, planned hikes and even a helicopter ride that toured ancient Indian ruins built into the mesas and hidden from common view. It was nothing short of a week of spiritual renewal with spa treatments, beautiful sunsets, fabulous food, and a lot of handholding and lifting up of sweet and cherished friends.

The first day of the actual trial, while driving on the way to hike through some ancient Indian ruins, the two of us friends told our hurting friend that we would do whatever was needed that day to get her through it. She just needed to say the word! At one point, we stopped for a restroom break at a drugstore and she began to fall to pieces. She literally began to unravel before our eyes. She went in to the store and came out with a cheap bottle of wine (she was never really a drinker) and I, being fairly familiar with good wines, tasted it and about choked! It tasted like cough syrup or worse! I said, "No, honey... if you're going to drink your way through this day, we're getting you something far better than this!" In short order, we indulged in snacks that would normally never pass through our calorie-conscious lips, and some wine that would have made my Napa friends envious. We sat in the parking lot while she shook in our arms and sobbed out all the pent-up anxiety, hurt, disappointment, and fear.

As it turned out, in the end, the lawsuit was settled. My friend and her husband were able to do the hard and admirable work of putting their marriage back together better and stronger than before. She never had to discuss the situation with her children, and the community never missed a beat.

Later, she asked how she could ever repay the two of us for holding her so closely through that week. I reminded her of the times when she had listened for hours to my own woes with my marriage, teenagers, parents, etc. I told her (and truly believe) that there is no scorecard between true friends, and that helping her had most definitely helped and renewed me. In my busy life, it took another friend's crisis to force me into the mountains, into my spirituality and my humanity. I've been better for it ever since and keep more balance in my life because of our time together.

It's like money in the bank, too, in a way. I know without a doubt that whatever the world dishes out to me in the future, she will be there with bells on, no matter what! That's the way it works. If I'm lucky enough to never need her in that way, what a great week it was in Sedona, and how great was that wine, anyway?

How far you go in life depends on your being tender with the young,
compassionate with the aged, sympathetic with the striving and
tolerant of the weak and the strong—because
someday in life you will have been all of these.
~ George Washington Carver

AFFIRMATION

I will be aware of my feelings and care for others today as I seek out those in need of my gift of love- whether they are young, old, successful, or disadvantaged. I know that I will contribute to the flow of love through the universe, and believe my energy will make a difference.

Today! I am **grateful** for:

_____
_____
_____

Today! I **intend** to contribute love to the universe and share one kind act with someone I come in contact with.

Today! My **"HEROIC MOMENT"** was:

_____
_____
_____

When I shared my gift of love, I **felt:**

_____
_____
_____

Day 7

KINDNESS FROM A STRANGER

by Erika Christensen

My mom passed away November 5, 2006. She was a coura-geous, generous person who would do anything for a friend. She was someone you wanted on your side. We had a very close rela-tionship; I was devastated when she died. She helped me become the person I am today. I try to be courageous, and generous, and I will do anything for a friend. That being said, my story starts here.

On a cold day about two weeks after my mom passed away, my family was getting ready to move from Texas to Nevada in about four weeks. My husband had already moved to start his new job. I never felt more alone in my life. When my mom was diagnosed with terminal cancer my friends called constantly, seeing how I was, if I wanted to meet for coffee or go to lunch. But I guess death makes people uncomfortable because, when I got home from her service in California, the phone stopped ring-ing. Was it because I was moving, or did they not know what to say? I was a wreck already, having to imagine my life without my mom, and now I felt like my friends had abandoned me. I am fiercely devoted to my friends and expect the same from them.

I was sitting in the bathtub feeling alone while my kids were in school. My mom was the person I could always talk to, and now she was gone. How was I going to manage? The phone rang and I recognized the name on caller ID. Though I never met her, I knew she was in the PTA. I thought, *what on earth does the PTA want me to do now?* I let the call go to voicemail and relaxed a bit longer. But soon enough my curiosity got the better of me and I checked the message. Her name was Jennifer. She was in the PTA but that was not why she called. She said she had heard my mother had just passed away. She wanted to talk to me because her mother had passed away that July. She said she knew what I was going through and if I ever wanted to talk to give her a call. Before saying goodbye she told me I was in her thoughts and prayers.

I wasn't alone. Someone else knew exactly what I was feeling! I sat in the bathtub and cried. I didn't feel so lonely anymore; I felt hope. A total stranger reached out to me and made my day brighter. I tried calling her back and got her voicemail. About a week later I was working at a festival at my kids' school, and she was there. She ran up to me and asked if I was Erika. I said yes and she gave me a huge hug. She told me who she was and we chatted for a while. She wished me luck with our move and we said goodbye.

We were in Reno for about two weeks when a card came in the mail from Jennifer. I have no idea how she got my new address. In the card she said she was thinking of me and how I was doing with the holidays and missing my mom. She gave me her address and phone number and told me if I ever wanted to talk to contact her.

I wrote her that day and told her how she touched my heart and how grateful I was. She took the time to reach out to a total stranger to say, "I know what you're going through. You are not alone."

Jennifer's generosity taught me about friendship. How important it is to be a good friend. It's not always easy or comfortable. When your friend is not feeling well, ask them if they need anything at the store. If something great happens in their life, celebrate with them. If they are feeling down, see if they want to go to a movie. If they lose a loved one, call them up to see if they're okay, if they want to meet for coffee or go to lunch. Even if you don't know what to say, being there says enough.

Real generosity is doing something nice
for someone who'll never find out.
~ Frank A. Clark

AFFIRMATION

Today will be fun as I will give an act of love anonymously. I will relish in knowing that I touched someone's life without them knowing it was me. This is love in one of its finest forms. I will enjoy the opportunity to participate in making someone feel loved.

Today! I am **grateful** for:

_____
_____
_____

Today! I **intend** to contribute love to the universe and share one kind act with someone I come in contact with.

Today! My **"HEROIC MOMENT"** was:

_____
_____
_____

When I shared my gift of love, I **felt**:

_____
_____
_____

Day 8

EMPTY NEST NO MORE

by Melissa Noethen

*I*t's funny how when you help someone it ends up blessing you so much more! My husband and I finally had the house to ourselves after sending our fourth child off to college. We had struggled for so long raising our four amazing children and saw a little financial light at the end of the tunnel when number four was well on her way. We started envisioning what could finally be done around the house and all the traveling we could start doing, etc.

Instead, we received a phone call one afternoon from my niece begging us to come across town to be with her. I had not heard from her in a couple years-- my sister had suffered severe depression after my brother-in-law committed suicide. She had gone into "hiding," shying away from us and throwing herself head first into a vicious and destructive journey of drug abuse. I knew things were bad, but did not realize how bad until I heard from my niece that day. You see, my niece was in labor (I didn't even know she was pregnant), and she was all alone. She was seventeen, homeless, and terrified.

My husband and I went to be with her at the hospital and watched little Alexa enter the world. The rest became a miracle journey for all of us. We brought my niece and her baby home with us from the hospital and cared for them for four-and-a-half years. We helped my niece deal with her traumatic childhood, taught her how to be a mother and how to break unhealthy behavior cycles. We found counseling for her, taught her to drive, cook, study, and work. Our children now consider her their own sister and niece, and my husband and I are "Nini and Papa" to this amazing four-and-a-half-year-old who we consider our granddaughter.

It has been really tough at times, and often overwhelming! But we have also experienced so much joy! This has healed the pain of losing my sister for both me and my niece. Watching Alexa grow healthy and happy is the greatest gift of all.

To acquire love…fill yourself up with it until you become a magnet.
~ Charles Haanel

AFFIRMATION

I know that to have an abundance of love in my life I need to share it with others. I will trust the law of attraction: the more I give, the more I will attract and enjoy in my own life. I will be aware and appreciative of the love that I attract into my life.

Today! I am **grateful** for:

_____

_____

_____

Today! I **intend** to contribute love to the universe and share one kind act with someone I come in contact with.

Today! My **"HEROIC MOMENT"** was:

_____

_____

_____

When I shared my gift of love, I **felt:**

_____

_____

_____

Day 9

VIRGINIA MIRACLE

by Ruth Trout

In late June I had MRI; a mass was found in my brain. I had three doctors' opinions before deciding surgery was the only option. My husband and I have three small children and had just started a business the previous year. We were scared to death. The procedure called for a craniotomy, an ear-to-ear incision and removal of the brain mass.

My mother-in-law offered to come for as long as she was needed. But she had not been at the house even twelve hours when she told me she wasn't going to be able to stay the three weeks she originally thought; actually she wouldn't even be able to stay a week. She was worried about her husband's health (he has diabetes). I booked a return flight for her for two days after my second surgery. I would still be in the hospital a week after that.

I called my best friend from home (Virginia) and told her how floored I was that my mother-in-law could do this to us! My own mother had not stepped up to do anything even though she lives in our town. I was really at a loss. My girlfriend said she would "take care of it." I later learned that she contacted my other best friend in Virginia and together they made plans to leave their own families and children to come and take care of mine. They stayed almost two weeks. It was incredible! In addition, my office manager, who has also become a very dear friend, basically took over my business – she did not skip a beat and never once called me. Yet another dear friend juggled her schedule to take my kids to school, soccer, football – you name it! She also came almost every night to visit me at the hospital. Oh, and did I mention that my school PTA brought us dinner every night for a month?

The surgery went great, I'm recovering really well, but these ladies just went so far above the typical "Call me if you need anything" that most people say when someone is having a difficult time – ME INCLUDED.

Well, I will tell you, I will never ever walk away from someone I know is in need without helping. I will not just offer to help; I'll help!

When we feel love and kindness toward others, it not only makes others feel loved and cared for, but it helps us also to develop inner happiness and peace.
~ The Dalai Lama

AFFIRMATION

I believe that my life is good. I am grateful for this new day and know that it is a gift to enjoy. I have the power to make today meaningful, and I will find the best in all situations. I will do nice things for others and know that my contribution to the world by giving kindness will bring inner happiness and peace to my own life.

Today! I am **grateful** for:

_____
_____
_____

Today! I **intend** to contribute love to the universe and share one kind act with someone I come in contact with.

Today! My **"HEROIC MOMENT"** was:

_____
_____
_____

When I shared my gift of love, I **felt:**

_____
_____
_____

Day 10

SHADOWS OF LOVE

by Sherry Striegel

It was never my mother's choice to move our family any one of the thirteen or so times we moved during my eighteen years at home. She would have preferred to make a home for us in one place. Nor was it a choice to raise my sister, brother, and me essentially as a single parent while my father traveled for a living. I remember Mom's stories of being at home alone with all three of us in diapers at the same time. She gave up everything to take care of us. She never talked about her dreams; she left a career behind as well as an unfinished education. The sacrifices were too many to count. Yet never once do I recall a complaint or even a tear. My mother is the epitome of strength and faith. She taught us through her example to deal with what life throws at you with grace and dignity. She learned how to live her life completely in the moment and not dwell on what might have been.

If Mom was the rock in our family, I was the complete opposite. I cried often and did not cope well with the constant state of upheaval and chaos in our family. I was the labeled the emotional one and, looking back, I suppose I was. I needed my mother's shadow as a shelter to get me through the turbulence. Without her quiet strength and even stronger faith, I would not be the woman

I am today. I hoped to someday be able to show her how much she meant to me. That day came unexpectedly, and in the face of one of the most tragic events in our family's life.

My mom's youngest sister, Debbie, a spitfire through and through, went to the doctor several years ago complaining of stomach cramps, among other pains. She was diagnosed with terminal cancer. Her life slipped away just weeks later. For many reasons, I was the only one of my siblings to attend Aunt Debbie's wake. I was often the butt of Aunt Debbie's barbs and teases, but I knew I needed to go. A moment that would forever define my relationship with Mom occurred at the service. She stood next to me clutching my hand so tight that I couldn't feel it. Our rock, the woman who I hadn't seen cry in twenty-five years, wept uncontrollably. She never let go of my hand. It was as though she needed for me to be a source of strength for her while, for that day, she completely let all her emotions overcome her. I can remember feeling the depth of the moment and the honor of being the one of her children who was there for her in her greatest time of need.

I had never seen my mom cry the way she did that day, and haven't seen her cry at all since. But on that day, just maybe I was there for her the way she had been for me all those years ago, able to stand in my shadow, a shadow of my unconditional love for her that is impossible to express in words.

Your vision will become clear only when you look into your heart.
Who looks outside, dreams. Who looks inside, awakens.
~ Carl Jung

AFFIRMATION

I know that I create my own reality and will take time today to listen to my soul and hear the voice of my heart. I know the universe supports what I believe, and I will choose to live in harmony with quiet whispers that guide me through my day. I will embrace all that I see as I look through the eyes of love.

Today! I am **grateful** for:

_____

_____

_____

Today! I **intend** to contribute love to the universe and share one kind act with someone I come in contact with.

Today! My **"HEROIC MOMENT"** was:

_____

_____

_____

When I shared my gift of love, I **felt**:

_____

_____

_____

Day 11

AN ACT OF KINDNESS RETURNED

by Linda Miles

*I*n 1998, a young dentist I met at one of our seminars had just purchased her first dental practice. She knew that the systems and many other areas of practice management needed to be changed. She invited me to join her practice as a consultant in late 1998. I knew the minute I met this young woman that she was going to not only be a great dentist, but also a wonderful client. I knew starting a practice was expensive and therefore gave her a $2500 reduced fee, subsequently forgetting that I had done so.

The practice grew and flourished. The team members she hired were loyal and dedicated to their doctor's new vision. The doctor attended the Pankey Institute and delivered the highest quality of care. By 2001, the practice had grown to the point that she needed a full-time partner. We kept in touch throughout the years with Dr. Deanna and her husband, celebrating my husband's and my fortieth wedding anniversary dinner in Sydney, Australia, in November 2001. She and her husband were in Australia visiting her brother, and I was there on a five-city speaking tour.

Lo and behold, in the summer of 2002, I received a beautiful letter that brought tears to my eyes. This wonderful client had sold half of her practice to her partner. She enclosed a check for

$2500, the long ago forgotten "gift" for the new dentist. Having always heard that returned gifts should be passed along to those less fortunate, I was able to surprise two of my favorite charities, those with special needs children, a gift of "pay it forward."

There are only two ways to live your life. One is as though nothing is a miracle. The other is as though everything is a miracle.
~ **Albert Einstein**

AFFIRMATION

I appreciate everyone and everything around me, and I will take note of all of life's treasures. Miracles are everywhere, and I promise to give someone a miracle through my own power and an act of love, and I will embrace the opportunity as it presents itself.

Today! I am **grateful** for:

_____

_____

_____

Today! I **intend** to contribute love to the universe and share one kind act with someone I come in contact with.

Today! My **"HEROIC MOMENT"** was:

_____

_____

_____

When I shared my gift of love, I **felt:**

_____

_____

_____

Day 12

THE SECRET

by CloAnn Christensen

"*I* have a secret!" my granddaughter, Chloe Tate, announced on her seventh birthday. Her eyes were sparkling, her smile was from ear to ear, and she couldn't stop moving. Yes, indeed she did have a secret.

Try as I did, she wouldn't even give me a hint. At seven, having a big secret is something special. I tried Twenty Questions, but obtained no clues. I even tried offering money for the information, but still she held her secret. (Of course, all this teasing was for fun because I knew this secret was the biggest secret in her whole life and eventually she would share -- in her own time and by her own choice.)

Chloe Tate is my namesake; we have always been close. Her beautiful, big brown eyes, sparkling smile, and tall, lean body make a grandmother very proud. I figured that she would at least tell *me* her secret. But nothing I said or did could break her resolve to keep this secret. The more I tried to be her confidant, the deeper she held her secret.

During the year, as she came to stay with me, I combed, brushed and styled her long, shining chestnut-brown hair. "Oh, what I would give for hair like that!" She accepted my comments and praise with an instant smile and dancing eyes. A week before her eighth birthday I received an email with two pictures. One showed Chloe and her long, long (by now really long) hair and one was Chloe with a new haircut. There was also a note telling me her secret!

During the previous year, Chloe heard about young girls who, through severe illnesses, had lost all their hair. This broke Chloe's heart. She felt there was something she had to do and *could* do, and that became her secret. She grew her hair long enough to be able to donate some of her hair to those girls! What a beautiful gift she gave of herself! Though she "lost" ten inches of her hair, she gained a thousand inches in character, love, and compassion. She gave more of herself than just her hair. She gave from her heart at the tender age of eight and touched the life of another.

Although Chloe is a young girl, she reminded me (at seventy) that there is no age limit to making a difference in this world. My granddaughter is my inspiration in making a difference for another person. As she "gave" her hair to Locks-of-Love, some beautiful young girl "received" a beautiful shining chestnut-brown wig. Both girls learned about a gift of love beyond what money could buy -- a secret gift from an eight-year-olds heart.

Miracles are instantaneous; they cannot be summoned, but they
come of themselves usually at unlikely moments
and to those who least expect them.
~ Kathleen A. Poter

AFFIRMATION

I will focus on the sweet moments that are invisible to the eye.
I know, in looking through the eyes of love, that miracles are seen
and opportunities presented. I will find them, as I know they are
out there waiting for me.

Today! I am **grateful** for:

_____

_____

_____

Today! I **intend** to contribute love to the universe and share one
kind act with someone I come in contact with.

Today! My **"HEROIC MOMENT"** was:

_____

_____

_____

When I shared my gift of love, I **felt**:

_____

_____

_____

Day 13

LITTLE CARDS

by Juliet Siddons

I went to college with a girl named Liz. We lived on the same fresh-man floor and joined the same sorority. Liz and I were never best friends or anything. But I always liked her and she was always very nice. Over the years we kept up with each through various friends. One day my husband came home from the golf course and asked if I new a girl named Liz from SMU. (Of course I did.) He proceeded to tell me that he had been playing golf with Liz's husband for a YEAR before they discovered in a conversation that their wives actually knew each other!

Soon after, my husband and I learned that Liz's mom had cancer. Liz's parents had divorced years earlier, so it was really just Liz and her mom (she had some brothers, but their relationships were nothing like the relationship between the mother and daugh-ter). Liz's dad even tried to do something – ANYTHING-- to help his wife. But nothing could be done. Liz's mother passed away about two years later.

Not quite a year after Liz's mother passed away, my own mother became ill with cancer. I cannot say that I did much of anything for Liz during her mother's illness. I did not know what to say or do for someone in that situation, and we still weren't really good friends or anything. However, as I was dealing with my mother's illness for eighteen months, every so often a little card arrived in the mail from Liz with a note saying she was thinking about me. I often told her how much those cards meant to me. She didn't seem to think it was anything, but I told her again and again how much it meant to me, especially since she had been through it herself. Knowing that she was thinking about me every so often made such a difference at that time.

We talked later after my mother passed and Liz said that maybe her own experience had happened so that she could be offer comfort to others. How gracious and wonderful is that? Liz still struggles with her own mother's death, I think more than most. I still see her pain every day; she has even admitted that the "joy" in her life seems to be gone. I hate that she suffers so much and feels so much pain. I now try to be a comfort to her as she was to me. I am truly blessed to have had someone like Liz be able to touch my life and help me through a very dark and difficult time, especially when it was so fresh and raw for her.

Miracles are unexpected joys, surprising coincidences, unexplainable experiences, and astonishing beauties…absolutely anything that happens in the course of my day, except that at this moment I'm able to recognize its special value.
~ Judith M. Knowlton

AFFIRMATION

I will notice the extraordinary in the ordinary today. Love is all around me. I will simply learn to recognize it.

Today! I am **grateful** for:

_____
_____
_____

Today! I **intend** to contribute love to the universe and share one kind act with someone I come in contact with.

Today! My **"HEROIC MOMENT"** was:

_____
_____
_____

When I shared my gift of love, I **felt**:

_____
_____
_____

Day 14

BIKINIS AND BIFOCALS

by Dr. Kim Westermann

All the women I know are busy, active, career women, me included. But for a long time my friend Diane and I had this drive to bring together our various circles of friends to share information, have fun and, in turn, help one another in some way. As we both faced turning fifty, our desire and need became stronger and stronger. Both being people who believe a positive attitude has had a tremendous impact on our lives, we became discouraged with the world's negative view of aging and even more determined to bring women together to purposely turn around that negative attitude about aging! That was when we started the Bikinis and Bifocals movement. The "Bikinis" is the attitude and the "Bifocals" is the reality!

Call us a support group for aging women -- or women who refuse to accept aging and will *never* grow old! We promote positive attitudes and images among women over forty. And, boy, has it taken off! So many women we meet love the fact that we put a positive spin on this stage of life for them. Life is what we make it, and we both work hard to change the attitudes and lifestyles of women so they can continue to lead active, fulfilled lives. As far as we are concerned, the best is yet to come. If we can't physically bring women together for fun and information, we created a website www.bikinisandbifocals.com for women to find and share information through our onsite forum. To read our personal story, just log on -- it's FREE!

Appreciation of life itself, becoming suddenly aware
of the miracle of being alive on this planet,
can turn what we call ordinary life into a miracle.
~ Dan Wakefield

AFFIRMATION

I recognize that I am here to make a difference in the world TODAY. It is my purpose. I will live in unison with the promise of today, and not the dream of tomorrow. I will feel appreciation for all that I have, for the sheer pleasure of it. It's a great day for a miracle!

Today! I am **grateful** for:

_____

_____

_____

Today! I **intend** to contribute love to the universe and share one kind act with someone I come in contact with.

Today! My **"HEROIC MOMENT"** was:

_____

_____

_____

When I shared my gift of love, I **felt:**

_____

_____

_____

Day 15

A FRIEND IN NEED

by Michele Inman

For more than ten years I enjoyed working with a lovely woman in my escrow office. We all loved her, and she was tremendously supportive of our entire team. One year following her retirement, she was given the tragic news that she had ovarian cancer. We were all devastated and deeply concerned.

Within weeks of getting the news, I received an email from one of my co-workers who was organizing a meal schedule for our sick friend's family. She was looking for anyone willing to provide meals for the family as often as possible while our friend was going through brutal and treacherous chemotherapy treatment. Our organizer's goal was to get as many days covered during the month as possible.

My own father was taken by cancer at the age of 65. I remember what the therapy involved and the toll it took on, not only my father but, all of our family.

Without hesitation, I signed up to bring in meals. My own life as a single, working mother with two active teenage boys was already overwhelming, over-scheduled, and financially challenging, but I knew I would have to find a way to make it happen.

I have provided meals to this struggling family once a month for several months. To be honest, sometimes it has been difficult due to my own work schedule and my sons' schedules. I'm usually running in so many different directions that adding one more demand on my day is a true challenge. But somehow I always seem to find a way to get a meal there, albeit oftentimes late! Once I get to their home, my stress dissolves, and I am filled with a wonderful sense of purpose. Whatever I endure during my demanding day can in no way compare to what this family is going through.

At such a sad and challenging time for this family, it makes me feel so blessed to play a small role in bringing a bit of sunshine and love to help ease some of their pain. With every meal, I am reminded of how blessed I am to have good health and to have the demanding and stressful life that I enjoy.

This family might go to bed with a full stomach from my once-a-month meal, but they give me a gift of going to bed with a full heart, knowing I had the opportunity to make a small difference in the life of someone who needed a little help.

* [Since submitting this story, Michele's dear friend lost her battle to cancer. Michele was able to speak with her the day before she passed because Michele listened to a small whisper that prompted her to call her friend that day.]

You control your future, your destiny. What you think about comes about. By recording your thoughts and goals on paper, you set in motion the process of becoming the person you most want to be. Put your future in good hands – your own.
~ **Mark Victor Hansen**

AFFIRMATION

There is a great deal of power in how I create what I want in life. I will be aware of all that I think about, and the control I have over what comes about during my day. I will choose who I want to be, and I will inspire others to do the same.

Today! I am **grateful** for:

_____
_____
_____

Today! I **intend** to contribute love to the universe and share one kind act with someone I come in contact with.

Today! My **"HEROIC MOMENT"** was:

_____
_____
_____

When I shared my gift of love, I **felt:**

_____
_____
_____

Day 16

WHEN YOU THINK YOU ARE STUCK

by Janice Hurley-Trailor

You know it when you see it -- that dull, glazed-over look in a woman's eyes. It's not anger; it's not resentment or distress. It's the telltale sign of having "checked out." It lives in the eyes of women who think they don't have any options and believe they are stuck. Many of us know that look because we have been there.

As a practice management consultant for a large orthodontic group in San Francisco, I worked once a month with the doctors and team members to organize and implement systems that would benefit everyone. I rotated my time between the three different offices and became more familiar with some members than others, of course.

One morning after some specific training with the administrative team on verbal skills, I noticed one of the young women had that look – that blank "I've given up" look. After the meeting I asked her to stay and talk with me a minute if she would. I let her know that she hardly knew me as I hardly knew her, and that she had no reason to trust that I would understand but would she please share her story with me? And she did.

She was twenty-six and a young mother of two. Her husband was on disability from a car accident, and she was their primary breadwinner. Her dream was to become a nurse. She had taken the necessary classes and passed her exams only to learn that her certificate would be held up until her school loans were paid. Unable to pay the more than eight thousand dollars needed, and not knowing where to turn, she had applied to join the Armed Forces. Distraught that she would be leaving her children, she was beside herself with self-disappointment and self-doubt.

I asked if she would be willing to trust me enough to call her debt collector and get a clear understanding of her financial position. When we did that, I learned that the original loan was for six thousand dollars, but she had incurred late fees and interest after graduating due to her inability to pay on time. I negotiated payment down to the original money borrowed minus late fees.

I told her that everyone has a time in their life when they are in a position to help others and a time to let others help them. Would she let me play that small role in her life right now by paying off her school loan? She did.

That quick transaction took place more then seven years ago. I couldn't tell you her name. She might not even remember mine, but I'll never forget the look when she came to work later to tell us she was leaving to take a position as a nurse in a nearby hospital. There was a smile on her face and, best of all, a light in her eye. This was one small act of kindness on my part towards a woman who just needed to know she wasn't stuck.

*You cannot control the world outside, but you can choose what you
will bring into yourself. If you do not see anything of value
in your life, begin by finding one thing of beauty
every day until it becomes a habit.*
~ Oprah Winfrey

AFFIRMATION

I will shift my focus and be willing to see everything around me in a new light. I acknowledge the beauty in the world around me – whether it is nature, people, architecture, or possibly even a delicious meal.

Today! I am **grateful** for:

_____

_____

_____

Today! I **intend** to contribute love to the universe and share one kind act with someone I come in contact with.

Today! My **"HEROIC MOMENT"** was:

_____

_____

_____

When I shared my gift of love, I **felt:**

_____

_____

_____

Day 17

SCRAMBLED EGGS

by Ruby Roof

*O*ne of the most touching moments in my life was when I had my first baby, Cole. I have a great friend, Karen, who offered to bring me dinner and to spend two or three hours with me at a time. She came and held my newborn so I could take a hot shower, eat a hot meal or take a nap. Karen had three young boys at the time, but she found someone to care for them so she could come to help me. I was so moved by her kindness and generosity. This gesture stuck with me as a fond memory from my first months of motherhood, which was a blur of hormones, sleep deprivation, a sore aching body, and painful side effects of breastfeeding for the first time.

One day, when she asked me what she could do while she was over, I asked, "Can you please scramble a couple of eggs for me?" A simple request, yes, but those eggs were the best scrambled eggs I can ever remember eating. I read in a pregnancy book once that while having a newborn, taking a hot shower can feel like a tropical vacation. For me, those hot scrambled eggs were like dining out at a gourmet restaurant!

Karen and other friends and family brought dinners and helped me again when I had my second child. These are such fond memories for me and the gestures will be with me for a lifetime. Since those days, I have taken on this gift of giving. When a friend or acquaintance has a new baby, I try to bring a hot meal. It is a wonderful tradition that I loved experiencing, and one that I hope to carry on for years to come.

When love is real, a miracle is produced.
~ Ernest Dimnet

AFFIRMATION

I am full of love. Therefore, I am full of potential miracles. I will share an act of love with someone who needs a miracle today. And I will be in tune to recognize the opportunity.

Today! I am **grateful** for:

_____
_____
_____

Today! I **intend** to contribute love to the universe and share one kind act with someone I come in contact with.

Today! My **"HEROIC MOMENT"** was:

_____
_____
_____

When I shared my gift of love, I **felt:**

_____
_____
_____

Day 18

PAY IT FORWARD

by Risa Simon

Seventy-two hours before I was to be on the platform to speak to a group of dentists in Gatlinburg, TN, my worst nightmare was upon me. I was forced to make a decision. Either show up sick or find a replacement. An SOS email was sent, which elicited an immediate response from the "queen" of speaking divas, the illustrious Linda.

"What part of Tennessee?" she asked. As I described the location, she incredulously picked up the phone to tell me that she and her husband Don were already planning on driving out to a neighboring town (just miles from the seminar site) on the day of the seminar. Mesmerized by her angelic voice and the uncanny synchronicities, she topped off the conversation by saying, "We'll simply leave a day earlier," which just happened to be the very next day!

Of course my next task was to sell the meeting planner on my replacement. After Linda's name was shared, there was a long silence on the other side of the phone. Was this, by a twist of fate, too good to be true? As I quickly discovered, it was not only true, it was about to get _even_ better! He said, "Truth be known, my committee actually had wanted Linda all along – they'll be thrilled to hear the news!"

I couldn't have dreamed a better scenario, if I had the screen-play rights! There was just one *much unexpected* moral dilemma I had to deal with when Linda refused to accept my honorarium. She said, "As dentists cover for their fallen colleagues and accept no money for doing so, I wish to do the same."

While I was more than moved by her generosity, I knew in my heart and soul that I could not accept such an offer. So, after plead-ing with her to comply with my wishes via *numerous* (and I mean numerous) emails, Linda finally surrendered – but not without a catch! Her acceptance was predicated on my willingness to "pay it forward" by becoming a Secret Santa to a short list of *very* special families "in need." And, a very special Secret Santa I became.

Just a few months down the line, (when I was convinced that I had heard and seen it all), a mysterious, (and quite substantial) check arrived from Linda. She claimed it was her "referral fee" for a client she met at the seminar in Gatlinburg. While my immediate response was to argue that her gift was outlandishly indulgent and unconventionally generous, I decided to reassess the situation and follow the trend that she so brilliantly initiated. Only this time my (all too familiar) acceptance speech had some Linda-ized strings attached!

"As a quick study of your teachings, I graciously accept your big-hearted gift, providing I can pay it forward to a research foun-dation that has the power to change the lives of over 12.5 million people worldwide." Thrilled to participate in yet another circle of kindness, Linda immediately re-issued the check to the PKD Foun-dation.

It's truly amazing how one email can lead to so many acts of human kindness. Thank you, Linda, for the profoundly gener-ous and loving spirit in which you serve; and for leading the path through the supremely magical world of "paying it forward."

We cannot live only for ourselves. A thousand fibers connect us with our fellow men; and along these fibers, as sympathetic threads, our actions run as causes, and they come back as effects.
~ Herman Melville

AFFIRMATION

I am mindful of the connection I have with each person I come in contact with. My actions will have an effect on the flow of love through the universe. I will find my purpose through sharing acts of kindness throughout my day.

Today! I am **grateful** for:

_____
_____
_____

Today! I **intend** to contribute love to the universe and share one kind act with someone I come in contact with.

Today! My **"HEROIC MOMENT"** was:

_____
_____
_____

When I shared my gift of love, I **felt:**

_____
_____
_____

AIRPORT ANGEL

by Nancy Austin

While on a business trip in Los Angeles, California, I received an alarming call from my son in San Jose, California, informing me that my daughter, Jody, had taken very ill and had just been admitted to the hospital. Being a single mom, this news set my entire being into panic mode.

I immediately phoned the airlines to get the first available flight to San Jose. I rushed to the airport, knowing it was going to be tight trying to make my flight on time. As I anxiously made my way to the check-in desk of the airline, I was informed that my flight was in the closing moments of boarding, and there was little probability I would make it to the gate in time.

This was prior to 9/11 and all the new security regulations. I frantically raced through the airport to my designated gate. I looked out the window; my pulse racing, my heart aching, and was relieved to see my plane. I cheered in my head, "I made it!"

The airline associate greeted me with a confused look as I leaned forward onto the counter and explained that it was imperative I get on that plane. She kindly explained that she was sorry, but the gate had already closed and the plane was cleared for departure. My heart dropped, and I began to sob uncontrollably. I attempted to compose myself. I told her that my daughter was very sick and had been admitted to the hospital a few hours prior, and I needed to get to her. In that instant she grabbed my hand and, before I knew it, we were both running feverishly down the ramp to the door. Sure enough, the door was closed and we both could see the plane starting to back away, about ten-to-fifteen feet already. She wrapped her arm around me, said she was sorry and that it was too late; there was nothing she could do.

I pleaded, "Please, you don't understand, I *have* to get on that plane!"

She immediately started waving her arms at the edge of the window, trying to catch the attention of the pilot. She finally caught his eye, but the pilot quickly waved her off. She didn't stop waving her arms. I didn't know at that moment if the plane had actually stopped, or if it was my desperate imagination, but the aircraft was soon moving toward us, rather than away from us. The associate put her arm around me and said, "Today is your lucky day my friend, looks like you're going to get on that plane after all."

One of the greatest sights in my life was watching the door of the airplane open. The flight attendant was obviously irritated, and she sharply directed me to quickly get on the plane. I wanted to hug and thank the assistant for all she had done for me, but I was already on borrowed time. I swiftly stepped onto the plane. I turned back to look at this woman, and with tear-filled eyes I mouthed the words, "Thank you!" She smiled and simply said, "Now go take care of your daughter." With the close of the airplane door, she was gone.

Hours later, I was by my daughter's side, holding her hand and feeling overwhelmed with love for her, as well as for the love and help of a complete stranger. I do not know the name of the woman who helped me, and I have never seen her again. But I will never forget her. She was my angel on that difficult day. I will always be so grateful for her going the extra mile to assist a stranger in desperate need.

Watch your thoughts; they become words. Watch your words; they become actions. Watch your actions; they become habits. Watch your habits, they become character.
~ **Daily Inspiration 1/20/05**

AFFIRMATION

I know that my thoughts are very powerful. They influence how I go about my days. I will be aware of old thoughts that have formed into habits, and I will patiently and diligently make the shift to creating positive thoughts when needed.

Today! I am **grateful** for:

_____

_____

_____

Today! I **intend** to contribute love to the universe and share one kind act with someone I come in contact with.

Today! My **"HEROIC MOMENT"** was:

_____

_____

_____

When I shared my gift of love, I **felt**:

_____

_____

_____

FURRY FRIENDS

by Maria Perno Goldie

We just returned from two weeks in Spain, and our beautiful Irish setter, Clancy, was so happy to see us. He had been cared for by our neighbors, Amy and Jerry, and their young twins, Haley & Rachel, while we were away. He had been playing in the cul-de-sac with our neighbor's grandchildren, eating well and generally enjoying life. Twelve hours after we returned, our beautiful best friend passed away on our floor, most likely from a stroke. My husband George and I called Amy and the girls, and we cried together.

At the time, Scooter, Amy's poodle, was six months old. Every day Amy called to ask if I would "babysit" Scooter. As Clancy did, Scooter had access to both of our backyards, and he had a doggy door at his house. Since it was summer, I kept our back door open so he could come and go. After about five days, I said to my husband, "I don't know why Amy asks me to watch Scooter, as he can come and go as he pleases."

George asked, "Haven't you figured it out yet? She is not doing this for Scooter; she is doing this for you."

I was so grief stricken that I was not thinking clearly.

It still brings tears to my eyes and, to this day, Amy and her family share their three dogs with us (as we travel too much to have our own dog). Such an act of friendship and kindness will never be forgotten. We now feel like grandparents to their three furry friends and, of course, we spoil them rotten!

We drop like pebbles into the ponds of each others' souls,
and the orbit of our ripples continues to expand,
intersecting with countless others.
~ Joan Borysenko

AFFIRMATION

My life becomes more meaningful when I choose to embrace love. I understand there is no safety or benefit in withholding love from myself or others. I will share my passion and energy with someone who needs to be lifted up.

Today! I am **grateful** for:

_____
_____
_____

Today! I **intend** to contribute love to the universe and share one kind act with someone I come in contact with.

Today! My **"HEROIC MOMENT"** was:

_____
_____
_____

When I shared my gift of love, I **felt:**

_____
_____
_____

Day 21

THE CIRCLE OF GIVING
AND RECEIVING

by M.J. Ryan

I was leading a mind/body/spirit fitness retreat with a friend. She'd brought along several other women to back us up logistically. Facilitating such events is very intense—we hike in the a.m., hold group sessions in the late afternoon, and individual sessions in between and in the evenings. I dropped into bed each night vibrating with fatigue.

One evening, I was sitting with one of the organizers who I knew only slightly. But I knew Naomi was a wise woman from the conversations we'd had in the past. She was telling me about a method for dealing with challenges that I had never heard of before. The words popped out of my mouth, "Will you do it for me?" I was thinking about my bag-lady fears that had proved resistant to everything I'd tried. "Sure," she said and we arranged a time.

We sat together in her room and, in thirty minutes, she helped me see and resolve things I had been stuck on for thirty years. I left feeling unbelievably blessed by her enormous kindness. She'd given to me what I have spent my life giving to others. All week I'd been the "wise" one, the one twenty-five women consulted about their problems, just like I am all day long at home. Now I was on the other side. It felt right to be part of the great circle of giving *and* receiving, to remember I need support and guidance too. Thank you, Naomi.

I have one life and one chance to make it count for something...I'm free to choose what that something is, and the something I've chosen is my faith. Now, my faith goes beyond theology and religion and requires considerable work and effort. My faith demands – this is not optional—my faith demands that I do whatever I can, wherever I am, whenever I can, for as long as I can, with whatever I have, to try to make a difference.
~ Jimmy Carter

AFFIRMATION

I choose to live fully today. I choose to embrace all that this day brings, and will share my love knowing I will make the world a better place today.

Today! I am **grateful** for:

_____
_____
_____

Today! I **intend** to contribute love to the universe and share one kind act with someone I come in contact with.

Today! My **"HEROIC MOMENT"** was:

_____
_____
_____

When I shared my gift of love, I **felt**:

_____
_____
_____

Day 22

MY NEW BEST FRIEND

by Gerda Christensen

In 1951, I was invited to attend an unfamiliar church in my home city, Aalborg, Denmark. At that time, I knew very little about my own religion, but was searching for a deeper level of inspiration. I decided to accept the invitation to attend church services the following Sunday. There I met a sweet and loving woman, Oda, who befriended me.

At that time I was a single parent struggling with three young children, and I had just been accepted to a six-month nurses training program. My youngest son, however, was not yet school age and needed daycare; I didn't know what to do with him during my training.

I mentioned my dilemma to my new friend, and she immediately offered to take care of him. I didn't know her very well, but there seemed no alternative. Still, I was worried about my son's welfare. For several days, I spent my lunch hour lurking around Oda's home, listening through the door to hear if he was crying.

Oda and her husband were very busy. They owned a little milk store and were raising six children. Every morning she arose early to get milk from the farmers. Despite her own responsibilities, she was a wonderful babysitter for my son. At the end of my training

I approached her to pay for her services. All she said was: "What I have done for you, you will be able to do for someone else."

Her goodness really touched my heart. At a time when I had no one to turn to, she gave me the greatest gift of love. Many times during the next year, I rode my bicycle past the stone houses that lined the streets to her house where we sat in her kitchen with fresh flowers on the table and had wonderful conversations. We became the best of friends during that time. Fifty years later, we still remain best friends.

A lot of people are waiting for Martin Luther king or Mahatma Gandhi to come back—but they are gone. We are it.
It is up to us. It is up to you.
~ **Marian Wright Edelman**

AFFIRMATION

Today is worth living. Today is worth giving. It is up to me to make the world a more loving place. I am responsible for giving my positive energy to the universe.

Today! I am **grateful** for:

_____
_____
_____

Today! I **intend** to contribute love to the universe and share one kind act with someone I come in contact with.

Today! My **"HEROIC MOMENT"** was:

_____
_____
_____

When I shared my gift of love, I **felt**:

_____
_____
_____

BINGO!

by Ann Mason

$\mathcal{I}$t was the summer of 1975, a time to rest from teaching and taking vacations with my family. Our next-door neighbors had in their home a refugee family from Vietnam, a family with two young children, Kathy and Bobby, who spoke absolutely no English. As a mother and a teacher, I knew I had to help Ling, the mother, with her children. Something had to be done to help them prepare for school in September, or else these children would struggle.

I offered to tutor the children in English for the summer. I could see Ling's excitement and concern at the same time. She didn't know me from anyone, and I'm sure didn't understand completely why a stranger was willing and wanting to help her children. But with Ling's hesitant approval, and my concerns of how I would communicate with these children, we jumped into the first day of English class at my kitchen table.

The only communication between Kathy, Bobby, and myself was their "fluent" and my "stumbling," high-school French. But a trust was soon built between us. They needed to learn as much English as possible in the next two months, and they needed my help.

We set a means of instant communication. If they did not understand a concept, we reviewed, re-attacked and tried again until

Kathy or Bobby could finally comprehend a given sentence, and they would respond with "Bingo."

Our first lesson together began with "The Gingerbread Boy." Kathy and Bobby knew the phonetic sounds from their excellent French and were able to read the words; it was the comprehension that was so difficult. "And the gingerbread boy ran on, and on, and on."

With puzzled looks they stared at me. What to do? We took hands and began to walk and walk, walking all around the house -- "on and on and on." After a minute or two they suddenly began chatting in Vietnamese and then, with sparkling eyes, they both said, "BINGO!"

And so began our English comprehension lessons.

It took these two beautiful young children only a couple of months; they were reading, comprehending, talking and sharing in English and laughing all the time. What a wonderful experience. I made some very special friends that summer, and they gave me back as much as I gave them. It was a time I will never forget.

They eventually moved out on their own, and I lost track of them. Years later, I received a wonderful surprise call from Ling. She wanted to share with me the exciting news that Bobby had graduated college with a doctorate in chemistry, and Kathy earned her M.D.

To think that I played a small role in helping them get started on their new journey in America gives me incredible joy. Now, that's a BINGO!

If you were alone in the universe with no one to talk to, no one with which to share the beauty of the stars, to laugh with, to touch, what would be your purpose in life? It is other life, it is love, which gives you meaning. This is harmony. We must discover the joy of each other, the joy of challenge, the joy of growth.
~ Mitsugi Saotome

AFFIRMATION

I am thankful for the opportunity to share my life with those I live with, work with, and have as neighbors and family members. The relationships in my life are what give me greater purpose. I will reach out to one of them and express my appreciation.

Today! I am **grateful** for:

_____
_____
_____

Today! I **intend** to contribute love to the universe and share one kind act with someone I come in contact with.

Today! My **"HEROIC MOMENT"** was:

_____
_____
_____

When I shared my gift of love, I **felt:**

_____
_____
_____

A WEDNESDAY TO REMEMBER

by Kathy Anderson

As a single working mother with full custody of two little girls, I was struggling to hold it all together while trying to get through the difficult rollercoaster and loneliness of a divorce. I felt a great sense of new independence, but I also felt more alone than ever before.

I was having a typical chaotic Wednesday -- dropping the girls off to school and hurrying to my office where I was to give an important presentation to a potential client our company was trying to land. The presentation went well, and I quietly celebrated my success as I plopped into my chair at my desk. What a great day I was having! Shortly thereafter, I checked my cell phone. Assuming it was my mother, I listened in surprise as I quickly realized the message was my daughter's school calling to tell me my youngest daughter, Claire, was very sick and that I needed to come pick her up immediately. I looked at the time of the call, and it was almost two hours prior. As I nervously dialed the school, feeling guilty from my irresponsible behavior as a mother, I was so surprised when the office administrator informed me that a friend of mine, Ann, who was also a working single mother, (and on my emergency call list) had picked Claire up over an hour ago.

I called Ann without delay and discovered that she had left her office immediately after receiving the call from the school. She was at her home with Claire. She told me "not to worry," and that I didn't need to hurry to pick her up as she had brought work home with her. Claire was sound asleep in her bed.

As I was driving to Ann's home to pick up my daughter, I was overcome with gratitude for this friend who left her own job to take care of my ill daughter. As I tried to express my appreciation when I got to Ann's home, she acted like what she had done was no big deal at all that she was happy to help!

That day was the last day that I felt alone in the world. I knew that people were out there who cared about me and were there for me if I needed them. I never had the opportunity to return the favor to Ann, but there have been other opportunities through the years that I've been able to step up and help someone in need. I never hesitate to do so, always thinking about Ann's kindness on that Wednesday during my own time of need. Her act of giving was not a big deal to her, but was an incredible gift to me. I'm sure she never thinks about that day, but I will never forget it.

The greatest things in your life happen in a moment. If you are not in the moment, you miss everything.
~ Lynn V. Andrews

AFFIRMATION

I know that miracles can happen in a moment. I will look for those moments today, and I will appreciate the new awareness of being able to recognize them all around me.

Today! I am **grateful** for:

_____

_____

_____

Today! I **intend** to contribute love to the universe and share one kind act with someone I come in contact with.

Today! My **"HEROIC MOMENT"** was:

_____

_____

_____

When I shared my gift of love, I **felt**:

_____

_____

_____

Day 25

REALTOR, MENTOR, FRIEND

by Heidi Bush

I have a beautiful story to share about my dear friend Helen. She changed my life and so many others'. She will have a special place in my heart forever.

Helen, a retired schoolteacher and successful Realtor in Pleasanton, California, was my mentor, my friend, and gift in my life. Knowing I was not happy in my career as a human resources director, Helen steered me to becoming a Realtor. Real estate was the furthest thing from my mind, but she saw things differently. She said, "Heidi, I am tired of selling you houses, YOU need to become a Realtor!" I asked her how I would do it, and she told me not to worry; she would take care of everything.

Before I knew it, I was signed up for school and riding in the car to show properties and open houses. She walked me through my learning process, and took the time to shape my life and career. She listed and sold all my properties and helped shape my career as a Realtor. I can never thank her enough. Helen's positive energy and continual support toward me is the reason I am a successful Realtor. Her judgment is perfection to me, and her way with people would make you melt with the kindness of her sincere approach of helping others in any shape or form. I love that about her and have used her example in my life so many times.

She is always there to pat my back, help in sorrow, laugh out loud, or eat a good meal and share good conversation. Most of all, I love her just because she is the "Shape of my Life" that I will treasure forever. I am lucky I have her. She is why I love, I work, and I cherish my friends.

When I dare to be powerful, to use my strength in the service of my vision, then it becomes less and less important whether I am afraid.
~ Audre Lorde

AFFIRMATION

I am connected to the power within me, and I will offer a gift to the universe today. With one small act, the ripples of love will begin and continue to flow until they reach the outer shore.

Today! I am **grateful** for:

_____

_____

_____

Today! I **intend** to contribute love to the universe and share one kind act with someone I come in contact with.

Today! My **"HEROIC MOMENT"** was:

_____

_____

_____

When I shared my gift of love, I **felt:**

_____

_____

_____

Day 26

MOTHER'S ADVICE

by Carol A. Dawson

About five years ago, I was extremely unhappy in my job with all the red tape that kept me from ensuring that all employees in our federal agency were treated fairly and equally. After twenty-five years of service in the government, an across-the-board early retirement was offered to anyone with (drum roll) twenty-five years of service. I had three months to make my decision. My plans were to start my own training and consulting business to work on equality without the red tape. I grappled with this decision every minute of every day and prayed for a sign from above...a burning bush, the Ohio River parting, anything! Those things didn't happen, but what I didn't recognize was that the signs were all around me. If I had listened to what people were saying, I would have known my destiny, but it wasn't until I was on the telephone with my mother, Glendene Baker, that I saw my direction; it was made loud and clear.

My mother asked me if I had made a decision. I told her no, but I had to make it in three days or the offer would be gone and I would have to work another nine years to get retirement. I was nearly in tears, worried about what to do when my mother very wisely gave me a gut-check. She asked me to think about the day after

I have made my decision not to take the retirement and imagine 5:45 a.m. and the alarm going off to get me out of bed. I imagined that morning and immediately felt a strange sensation. My mother then asked me how I was feeling. I told her I felt ill and my stomach was churning. I could hear her smiling on the telephone as she said, "Carol, I think you know how you would feel if you lose this opportunity. Now ask yourself if this is the way you want to feel every morning for the next nine years."

It wasn't, and I now hold the dubious title of being the youngest, non-disabled person to "retire" from that federal agency. My Equal Employment Opportunity (EEO) business is strong, and every day I am grateful for my mother's caring advice and gut-check.

Each person's smile at a particular moment constitutes a unique event in the history of mankind.
~ Rene' Dubos

AFFIRMATION

I have the opportunity to smile at those I come in contact with. I will greet each person who crosses my path with a smile, knowing I could be changing their entire day.

Today! I am **grateful** for:

_____

_____

_____

Today! I **intend** to contribute love to the universe and share one kind act with someone I come in contact with.

Today! My **"HEROIC MOMENT"** was:

_____

_____

_____

When I shared my gift of love, I **felt:**

_____

_____

_____

Day 27

THREE MILES, THREE WOMEN

by Renita Bernat

This is a story about early mornings, three miles, and a world of difference. It is also about three women, the ability to listen, and the capacity to care.

There are three of us... there are really about twelve of us, both men and women, but on Tuesday and Thursday mornings, rather then the usual crowd of folks who run the same five-mile course that we've been running for twenty-three years, the three of us walk, talk and share our lives. It is like a rest day from the usual running routine. We started this "walk and talk" about four years ago. It has probably saved each of us thousands of dollars in therapy fees.

The issues have varied from aging parents to abstinent sons - or daughters-in-law. It's been about the death of a friend or the death of a relationship. It's been about weddings, babies, and grand babies. Most important, it's been about us.

Anybody can solve, resolve and advise, but it takes a special person to listen--just listen. Someone who will let you pour your heart out, cry, even wail if that's what you need to do. Just listen. There is magic in it.

There have been disagreements and misunderstandings among the three of us from time to time, but we have a respect for each other, and the time that we share, that makes this morning relationship one of caring and gratitude for its existence.

Every circumstance and situation gives you the opportunity to choose this path, to allow your soul to shine through you, to bring into the physical world through you its unending and unfathomable reverence for and love of life.
~ Gary Zukav

AFFIRMATION

I choose to live a life filled with love. I know the universe stands behind my desires. I will enjoy every opportunity to express my love and allow my soul to light up the lives of others.

Today! I am **grateful** for:

_____
_____
_____

Today! I **intend** to contribute love to the universe and share one kind act with someone I come in contact with.

Today! My **"HEROIC MOMENT"** was:

_____
_____
_____

When I shared my gift of love, I **felt:**

_____
_____
_____

Day 28

THE GIFT OF ABBY

by Anita Barton

I would like to share my experience with my thirty-eight-year-old niece Amy and her mother Linda (Linda and my brother have been divorced for many years). My brother, who was battling with cancer, had completed his chemo treatments locally. After his final treatment he was told there was nothing left to do, so he and his daughter Amy (his only child) decided to participate in a trial study at Sarah Cannon Institute for cancer in Nashville, Tennessee. After just one week there, he became very ill and was unable to complete the treatment. He wanted to come home to Louisville, Kentucky, to say goodbye to his family and friends and, especially, his dog Abby.

My brother's health was deteriorating quickly and Amy called on every hour to keep me updated. The family cousins (all very strong women) provided me with comfort during this ordeal, not knowing if my brother would survive the three-hour ambulance trip home. We sat waiting in the Louisville ER for his arrival, staring out the large floor-to-ceiling windows.

Finally, Amy called on her cell phone to say they were fifteen minutes away but that Jerry's blood pressure was dropping; he was getting weaker. The clock was ticking as we prayed he would hold on long enough to get to his room so we could all say our goodbyes. As I stared out the window, I noticed a large willow tree and a lady with a dog trying to hide behind the tree. I took a closer look and, to my surprise, it was Amy's mom. Linda had picked up Abby and brought her to the hospital so Jerry could say goodbye to his sweet dog. This brought laughter and tears to all our eyes. As the ambulance pulled up, we rushed to see my brother. What we saw was a very weak and fragile man, barely alive. His blood pressure was 68/40 when he reached out with both arms to hold his dog and kiss her goodbye. Amazingly, his BP started going up and, with his heartbeat stronger, the doctors were able to get him to his room so we could say our goodbyes. My brother passed away a few hours later.

I am so grateful we were blessed to have time with him, even enough time for my son to arrive from Chicago. I truly believe that the strength of Amy insisting that he be able to return home, and the kind act of Linda bringing Jerry's dog Abby, gave us the precious gift of time with my brother to say our goodbyes. My brother was able to pass on from this life with his loving family all around him.

Imagination is the beginning of creation. You imagine
what you desire; you will what you imagine;
and at last you create what you will.
~ George Bernard Shaw

AFFIRMATION

I know that just by imagining a life filled with love, I can create that desire by giving of love today. I have control of what I think and do, and I choose to make this a day one of touching someone's life with my POWER.

Today! I am **grateful** for:

_____

_____

_____

Today! I **intend** to contribute love to the universe and share one kind act with someone I come in contact with.

Today! My **"HEROIC MOMENT"** was:

_____

_____

_____

When I shared my gift of love, I **felt**:

_____

_____

_____

Day 29

FIFTY YEARS OF FRIENDSHIP

by Fran Pangakis

Carol and I have been friends since we were fours years old. Since I'm an only child, I look at her much more like a sister. Through the years we've both been through so much and, depending on who needs who at what time, we are always there for each other.

For a relationship that spans more than fifty years it's hard to pick just one story that talks about how we've been each other's support. What I remember the most though is all of the laughter we've shared together. There are times that we become those giggly teenagers again who had their lives in front of them. Even though now those years ahead are less, we still find at least one time when we are together where we find something so funny that we are in tears from laughter.

Sometimes it's not the talking that becomes powerful; it's knowing that you can always count of someone to just be there, even if it's sitting quietly together and just being.

Love is a central condition of human existence. We need it for survival; we seek it for pleasure; we require it to lend meaning and purpose to ordinary existence.
~ Williard Gaylin

AFFIRMATION

I find meaning in my every day by sharing love with those around me. It gives me pleasure and purpose, and touches those I give love to. Everybody wins when love is shared.

Today! I am **grateful** for:

_____
_____
_____

Today! I **intend** to contribute love to the universe and share one kind act with someone I come in contact with.

Today! My **"HEROIC MOMENT"** was:

_____
_____
_____

When I shared my gift of love, I **felt:**

_____
_____
_____

Day 30

COMING HOME TO TILLY

by Melinda Lawrence

I divorced after twenty-five years of marriage. During those years, I kept myself on the bottom of the list for TLC. Having grown up in the fifties and sixties, I learned at a very early age that, as a woman, sacrifice was what it was all about. Sacrifice yourself for the sake of those you loved.

After the divorce, my goal, struggle, and dream, was to learn how to "love myself." "Tilly" (my childhood nickname) had been on the bottom for so long, I didn't know how to begin to put her first. During counseling and reading every self-help book I could find, I discovered a method that was life-changing. I had to envision myself, as a grown-up, in a safe environment. Then, imagine Tilly, my inner child, talking to me and asking me for whatever she needed to feel safe and loved. I could see Tilly walking toward me-- her little brown dress, her long curly hair, just as I remembered from a picture I had seen. She came to me, sat on my lap, put her arms around me and began to cry. I slowly wrapped my arms around her (me) and began to sooth her and tell her how much I loved her (me). For the first time in forty-six years, I was *taking care of* Tilly, me. For the first time in forty-six years, I was *learning how to love* Tilly, ME!

The love I had so generously shared with others was finally coming home to me. Learning to love myself has given me the blessing of loving others even more.

To a loving person, everybody is worthy of love;
every occasion is an opportunity to practice love.
~ Eknath Easwaran

AFFIRMATION

I visualize love surrounding all those I see today. Because I am a loving person, I embrace the opportunity to give love at each encounter--whether this is a kind thought, words of encouragement, or simply a compliment.

Today! I am **grateful** for:

_____

_____

_____

Today! I **intend** to contribute love to the universe and share one kind act with someone I come in contact with.

Today! My **"HEROIC MOMENT"** was:

_____

_____

_____

When I shared my gift of love, I **felt**:

_____

_____

_____

CONCLUSION

$\mathcal{M}$ost of what we need to experience true happiness in life is simple, but that doesn't necessarily mean it's easy. Sadly, the majority of people would rather settle for mediocrity than go the extra mile to create fulfillment and joy in their lives. Genuine happiness is not that far away, but it does require a paradigm shift in how we approach each day. What have been shared throughout this book are simple guiding principles that give each day meaning and purpose and produce a transformation in our hearts.

We can either spend our lives searching for the meaning of life, or we can rewrite our beliefs and create it for ourselves. We change our personal experience in the world by changing the way we live in it. The answers to enjoying a fulfilling life are not found outside of us, they are found within us. Once we awaken and honor our authentic purpose, we realize our own capacity to love and be loved.

All the stories you have read in this book were submitted by women like you. If you were moved by this 30-day journey or any of the stories from the book and would like to share your own experiences and heroic moments, please forward them to carrie@ heroesinheels.com, or visit the website at www.heroesinheels.

com. Some of your stories will be shared in the next edition of *Heroes in Heels.*

Create and embrace the life you were truly meant to live and enjoy the beautiful journey! It will be whatever you make of it.

The finish line is just the beginning of a whole new race...

BOOSTER SHOTS

- Share a kind smile.
- Open a door for a stranger.
- Give a compliment.
- Pay for the person behind you in the toll line.
- Say "thank you."
- Send a card for no special reason.
- Donate any amount of money to charity.
- Call your mom.
- Say you're sorry.
- Let someone win.
- Give a flower.
- Kiss your child out of the blue.
- Hug your parents.
- Remember birthdays.
- Wish others a great day.
- Say "yes" instead of the usual "no."
- Tell the truth.
- Say a silent prayer for someone.
- Look into a strangers eyes and smile when you walk by them.
- Give a bigger tip than normal.
- Resist confrontation.

- Count to 10 before saying something when angry.
- Volunteer your extra time.
- Give a secret gift.
- Visit an elderly friend.
- Share good music with someone.
- Give what you don't need to someone who does.
- Buy a stranger lunch.
- Listen. REALLY listen.
- Do something you know you should but don't really want to.
- Hold someone's hand.
- Share your successes in order to help someone else succeed.
- Teach others something you have mastered.
- Share your talents.
- Squelch gossip.
- Spread good rumors.
- Speak kind words.
- Praise more often.
- Master patience.
- Ask for forgiveness.
- Be someone's cheerleader.
- Become a mentor.
- Give love unconditionally.
- Choose happiness on a day that you aren't feeling happy.
- Look for someone in need.
- Accept change.
- Work hard.
- Don't waste your time.
- Don't waste someone else's time.
- Be grateful to be of service.
- Honor differences.
- Choose tenderness.
- Laugh out loud.
- Make someone else laugh.
- Cry with someone who needs to cry.
- Leave a love note.
- Don't judge when it's easy to judge.

- Give constructive advice.
- Give something for nothing.
- Pay someone else's parking meter whose time has run out.
- Whisper sweet somethings.
- Take a compliment and say thank you.
- Accept a new idea.
- Release resentment.
- Challenge yourself.
- Challenge others to become more.
- Give someone a ride.
- Share your knowledge.
- Don't "keep the change," give it away.
- Strike up a conversation.
- Share positive quotes.
- Pass a good book along.
- Teach by example.
- Lose the negative.
- Slow down and take notice.
- Be a peacemaker.
- Resolve old angers.
- Call a long lost friend.
- Don't play games unless it's *Monopoly*.
- Mind your own business.
- Mind someone else's business when asked.
- Let someone vent.
- See the best in everyone.
- Let someone in line in front of you.
- Choose uplifting words.
- Keep it simple.
- Lose a bad habit.
- Be a leader.
- Be love.
- Share your candy.
- Ease someone else's burden.
- Turn words into action.
- Always keep a promise.

- Play with a child.
- Support a worthy cause.
- Believe someone else can achieve.
- Spread joy.
- Be someone's guardian angel.
- Give up your seat.
- Say "I LOVE YOU" really loud!
- Say it again!

ACKNOWLEDGEMENTS

*H*eroes in Heels has been a true labor of love. After three complete rewrites, endless hours of work, and what seemed like a never-ending task; I am honored and thrilled to share the final result. I wish to gratefully acknowledge the following:

First and foremost, I thank my loving husband and best friend, Rob Flintom, who has been my greatest supporter and cheerleader. You believed in my dream as much as I did. This book would not be finished today were it not for your endless emotional support, encouragement, and belief in me. You inspire me every single day to live authentically and passionately, to trust my inner voice, and follow my true north. Thank you for turning all my tears into stars. I love you beyond words. You are HIM!

To my three extraordinary children, Addison, Clark, and Karlie, thank you for all your love, support, unwavering trust in me, and encouragement in life and with this book. You are my life's greatest purpose and your love and belief in me has always been my strength. You have brought more joy and happiness into my life than I ever imagined possible. I feel honored, privileged, and thankful to be your mom.

A deep and heartfelt thank you to Pam Rundquist, my "sister under the skin" and collaborator on this project; the journey of our friendship and the conception of this book have been, and always will be, cherished in my soul. Together, we have been through some of the greatest highs and most painful lows of our lives. Only you know the breadth and depth of my personal journey and evolution, both emotionally and spiritually. If it were not for your beautiful love and friendship, I would not be where I am today. Thank you for all that you've helped me overcome, and become.

To my parents, Bjarne and CloAnn Christensen, who taught me by example the joy that comes from helping and serving others. Thank you for all your expressed love, confidence, and guidance throughout my life and especially for supporting me with this venture. I greatly appreciate all your assistance with reading and rereading this manuscript; providing invaluable feedback and insight, and helping me to see beyond the words when I was so immersed in this project that I couldn't see my way through the words.

To my brother, Kyle Christensen (my surrogate sister!), thank you for supporting and loving me unconditionally, especially during the challenging years I struggled to love myself, and for showing up (with guitar and really bad lyrics at times) when I have needed you the most. You are, and always have always been, my guardian angel.

To my brother, Knute Christensen, for all your love and support and for teaching me invaluable life lessons that I would never have learned otherwise, thank you for watching over me during our college years.

To Lisa Camera, my dear friend, your love, honesty, and support are priceless treasures in my life. Thank you for your continued encouragement and enthusiasm with this book. Although you stand tiny in stature, you are one of the strongest women I have ever known. You are a giant in how you live and love, and I feel honored to call you my friend.

In addition, my sincere appreciation for my friend and mentor, Katherine Eitel, who not only contributed a story, but kindly forwarded my email request for stories to her friends and business associates. Unbeknownst to her, a domino effect took place as women continued to forward her email, which resulted in many of the stories in this book. (You'll notice a few stories come from those in the dental profession) Although she has not met all of the women who contributed stories, many of them came to me indirectly through her. From the bottom of my heart, thank you Katherine!

Finally, to all the remarkable and inspirational women who shared their personal stories – you are the heartbeat of this book. May you continue to create a more fulfilling, supportive, purpose-filled, and loving existence for yourselves and for each other.

You are all the "Heroes in Heels" that inspire me to become more of whom I am meant to be.

With my love, appreciation, and deep gratitude,

Carrie

Carrie Flintom is a life coach dedicated to helping women live with passion, purpose, and meaning. She enjoys speaking to organizations to inspire, awaken, and ignite the human spirit. Carrie is passionate about bringing women together for connection and strength, while empowering them to appreciate and support one another in an entirely new way. Carrie is the mother of 3 grown children, and lives in San Diego, California with her husband.

Visit her website at www.heroesinheels.com.

For information about her life coaching or speaking services, contact Carrie directly at carrie@heroesinheels.com, or call 858-997-6305.